Published by
Cleveland Landmarks Press, Inc.
13610 Shaker Boulevard, Suite 503
Cleveland, Ohio 44120-1592
www.clevelandbook.com
(216) 658-4144

ISBN: 978-0-9367602-3-0

LIBRARY OF CONGRESS NUMBER:
2007934636

Designed by
John Yasenosky, III

Printed by
BookMasters, Inc.
Ashland, Ohio

# CITIZEN SOLDIERS:
## 107TH CAVALRY REGIMENT, OHIO NATIONAL GUARD

FACERE NON DICERE

### GEORGE N. VOURLOJIANIS

*Acknowledgements and Photo Credits*

## ACKNOWLEDGEMENTS AND PHOTO CREDITS

In October 2007 the First Cleveland Cavalry Association will be celebrating the 130th anniversary of its founding. More years ago now than I care to remember, one of my college history professors told us in class that anniversaries of events are the best times to write and get things published. This work is the result of that advice, coupled with a strong personal interest in the 107th Cavalry's history.

This book would not have been completed without the help, generosity, patience, and good will of a lot of people. First, I would like to thank the archivists and librarians, whose professionalism and expertise greatly contributed to the successful telling of this story: Lynn Duchez Bycko, Special Collections Associate of the Cleveland State University Library; Nan Card, Curator of Manuscripts at the Rutherford B. Hayes Presidential Center; William Stark, Archivist of the Cleveland Grays Collections; Elmer Turner of the Cleveland Public Library Photographic Collection; and Ann Sindelar, Reference Supervisor at the Western Reserve Historical Society. A special debt of gratitude and a "salute" to Staff Sergeant Joshua Mann, Archivist and Historian of the Ohio

Army National Guard. I would like to thank Brigadier General Thomas P. Luczyniski and Chief Warrant Officer George A. Ehrman and the members of the First Cleveland Cavalry Board of Trustees, and the veterans of the 107th Cavalry Regiment for their material and moral support. I also owe an enormous debt of gratitude to Dr. James Toman of Cleveland Landmarks Press whose editorial insights were tremendously valuable in completing the work. Finally, it remains for me to thank the colleagues and many friends who supported and encouraged my efforts; but above all my wife, Sally, who is always there for me.

The following list explains the source for each abbreviation used to identify photo sources in the text: Cleveland Grays Archives, *CG*; Cleveland Public Library, *CPL*; Cleveland State University, *CSU*; Donald J. Clink Collection, *Clink*; First Cleveland Cavalry, *FCC*; Frank J. Marinchick Collection, *FM*; Kent State University Library - Special Collections, *KSU*; Ohio Army National Guard Archives, *OANG*; Ohio Historical Society - Hayes Presidential Site, *OHS-Hayes*; Western Reserve Historical Society, *WRHS*.

George N. Vourlojianis
July 2007

Members of a city's socio-economic elite composed the ranks of many of the volunteer independent military companies. The First Cleveland Cavalry was such a unit. The troop roster included such men as John Hay. Hay had been President Lincoln's private secretary and later served as Secretary of State in the administrations of William McKinley and Theodore Roosevelt. *OHS-Hayes*

The son of President Rutherford B. Hayes, Webb C. Hayes was a founder of the Union Carbide Corporation. A troop member, he transferred to the Regular Army during the Spanish American War. He was awarded the Medal of Honor for action in the Philippines. Hayes is wearing the Troop's custom-tailored dress uniform, chasseur jacket, topped by a black bear-skin busby. *WRHS*

## INTRODUCTION

The American military tradition has its origins in Western Europe. In antiquity, the Greek city-states required all able-bodied, free men to come forth to defend their polis when summoned. Later during the reign of England's Alfred the Great all freemen or yeomen between the ages of 16 and 60 were required to bear arms in the defense of the kingdom. This obligation was known as the Saxon *fyrd*. It was the equivalent of a medieval militia.

In 1181 the English King Henry II issued the Assize of Arms. The Assize legally bound his subjects to come to the defense of the realm when called upon to do so. Henry II thus created a legal obligation by which the civilian was turned into a part-time — or citizen—soldier.

When the English colonized America, they brought with them their fear of a large standing army of regulars or professional soldiers. If misused, a professional army could become a powerful weapon in the hands of a tyrant. English history contained numerous examples of such abuses of armed power. King John, Charles I, Cromwell's New Model Army, and James II all in turn

Originally from Lorain County, Myron T. Herrick settled in Cleveland in the 1870s. An attorney, he first joined the Cleveland Grays and a short time later the First City Troop. He was one of the founders of the Cleveland Hardware Company and Union Carbide. He also served as chairman of the board of Society for Savings. Active in Republican politics, he was elected Ohio governor in 1903 and later served as ambassador to France. *WRHS*

A great deal of Cleveland's phenomenal wealth came from steel production and the associated iron ore mining industry. Prominent among the city's industrialists was Samuel Mather. Mather was a founding member of the troop and of Pickands Mather, the giant iron ore mining and Great Lakes steamship company. *WRHS*

had used the regular standing army to establish in one form or another a tyranny over the citizenry. It was this history that led the English to view a large standing army as ominous. This fear, along with the tradition of the citizen soldier, accompanied the settlers to the New World.

In the New World, the English colonists organized their own defense against Native Americans and European enemies. Local militia companies were formed in every settlement. A mighty struggle began in 1689 between England and France and their allies for the colonial and commercial domination of the globe. Between William of Orange's accession to the English throne and the defeat of Napoleon at Waterloo (1815), the two nations fought seven wars, filling 60 years and covering lands and oceans from the forests of western Pennsylvania to the jungles of India, and from the Caribbean Sea to the mouth of the Nile. In America, much of the fighting was done by colonial militias, but the immensity and importance of the struggle necessitated the sending of British regulars. At the end of the last colonial war in America, the French and Indian War, King George III did

Military encampments were held each summer. In 1888, Troop A traveled to Columbus for an Ohio National Guard state-wide training camp. *OHS-Hayes*

Setting up camp, troop members organize their gear and make up their bunks. Note the straw protruding from the tear in the mattress. *OHS-Hayes*

not withdraw his regulars. They remained in Canadian garrisons and on the frontier regions of the 13 colonies. A series of actions by Parliament designed to raise colonial taxes and restrain certain economic activities met with a violent reaction which resulted in the destruction of Crown property. In response to this lawlessness, the Crown shifted troops from Canada to the larger cities of the 13 colonies, most notably, Boston, New York, and Philadelphia. Reinforcements were also sent from the British Isles.

These actions on the part of Parliament and the Crown aroused historic fears of the regular army as a powerful weapon in the hands of a tyrant. It was in the mind of many colonists that King George III was attempting to deprive them of some of their fundamental English rights. In April 1775 blood was spilled during a skirmish in Massachusetts between the militia of Lexington and Concord and British regulars. The American Revolution had begun.

At the beginning of the Revolutionary War, the Continental Congress formed the Continental Army. Each colony (called states after July 4, 1776) raised a segment of the army. Responsibility

W. C. Hayes 2. M. Sergt.     H. C. Rowe 1st Sergt.
First Cleveland Troop - O. N. G. State Encampment - Columbus Ohio, 1888

A typical non-commissioned officer's tent. Standing trooper is leaning on his 1860 pattern cavalry saber. The two rifles are non-government issue Sharps Borchardt single shot .45-70 carbines. Both sergeants are wearing Mills pattern woven cartridge belts. Patented in 1881 by Brigadier General Anson Mills, each belt held up to 50 cartridges. *OHS-Hayes*

for raising, clothing, feeding, and paying the soldiers was the states' responsibility. These Continental units were separate from the militia. The militia provided home defense and was a source of manpower for the Continental army. George Washington, appointed commander by Congress, commanded the Continental army from early July 1775 through late fall 1783.

The traditions brought from England by the colonists, together with the necessity of self-defense and a determination to preserve democracy, resulted in a unique American military ethos. Responding to a request from Congress in 1783, George Washington wrote *Sentiments on a Peace Establishment.* With the approval of his Revolutionary War generals, Washington laid forth the foundations of the nation's defense. First and foremost among Washington's *Sentiments* was the establishment of a force of regulars that would be reinforced by the militia.

The causes of the Revolution were fresh in the minds of Americans. They feared a large standing army of regulars. When the Constitutional Convention met in Philadelphia in 1787,

"Rank hath its privilege." Officers and sergeants gather for mess call. Note the silver punch bowl and china on the table. *OHS-Hayes*

Dining in style. The troop is being served a meal in the field. *OHS-Hayes*

the delegates were very aware of this fear. By design, they created an army that would be under civilian control. The President is its commander in chief, and Congress provides its funding. In an effort to insure ratification and to allay the people's fears, Alexander Hamilton, John Jay, and James Madison published a series of pamphlets called *The Federalist Papers*. In these pamphlets they laid forth the argument that the military would be under civilian control and that there was nothing to fear.

The Constitution reflected Washington's opinions and those of many of his fellow countrymen when it authorized an army of regulars reinforced by state-controlled militias. The Militia Act of 1792 laid forth the rules under which the militia would function. Despite the passing of laws obligating citizens to military service, Americans generally had and still have an aversion for things military.

As a result of neglect, poor funding, and civilian apathy, the militia organization created by the Constitution existed only on paper. Therefore, to protect themselves from foreign invasion and domestic disturbances too great for the local police to deal

"An army travels on its stomach." Sutler delivering supplies to the camp. Civilian cooks and "strikers," or dining stewards, pose in the mess area. Civilians were contracted to perform "domestic" chores around the camp. *OHS-Hayes*

with, citizens throughout the country came together and organized themselves into independent volunteer military companies.

By the early nineteenth century, cities, towns, and villages throughout the country had established one or more of these independent military companies. Except for statutory recognition, these independent militias received no state support. Using their own money, the members armed and equipped themselves. Consequently, their ranks were generally drawn from the socio-economic elites of the community. Arms, uniforms, equipment,

and armories were expensive to procure and maintain.

Every active volunteer company also called for financial and moral support from local businesses and professionals whose property would be at risk during times of civil disturbance. The volunteer companies also created veterans' support groups that served as the military equivalent of an alumni association. Membership was nearly always by invitation, and new members were voted into the company. The style of their arms, equipment, uniforms, and company names were inspired by elite units in

11

Cavalrymen were armed with carbines, pistols, and sabers, in line here firing pistols. *OHS-Hayes*

By the end of the nineteenth century, the saber was considered by many military experts to be a quaint relic of the past. However, the cavalry still considered it their principal weapon. Troops "presenting sabers" during a drill. White trousers were sometimes worn during the summer. *OHS-Hayes*

European armies: dragoons, guards, grenadiers, light artillery, fencibles, and lancers.

The independent companies had a social side that made membership in them desirable. In many ways, they were gentlemen's military social clubs. They sponsored stag dinners, lavish military balls, and held excursions for themselves and their guests. In addition to entertaining themselves and their friends, they also provided a social outlet for the general community. On patriotic holidays and celebrations they paraded through the city streets. They sponsored band concerts, drill competitions, and to the awe and delight of onlookers, cannon-firing demonstrations.

Throughout antebellum America independent military companies flourished. To the roster of socially elite companies were added companies whose membership included mechanics, artisans, and volunteer firemen. During the same period, Irish and German immigrants, who were victims of a pervasive distrust on the part of those who were well established, were eager to demonstrate that they too were "good" Americans, and so these groups organized companies of their own.

Preparing to attack. With sabers drawn and at the ready, the troop is drawn up in the "attacking in line" formation. *OHS-Hayes*

## THE CIVIL WAR YEARS

The volunteer militias seemingly provided proof of the viability and reliability of the American citizen soldier as the bulwark of the nation's defense. These would be rigorously tested during the Civil War.

The most troublesome issue that the nation grappled with during its formative period was slavery. Northern anti-slavery factions known as abolitionists called for its immediate outlawing. Southerners viewed it as the very foundation of their unique political, social, and economic order. The end of slavery would be catastrophic to the white South. After several failed attempts at finding a political solution to this moral dilemma, Southern firebrands used the election of Abraham Lincoln to the presidency as an excuse for separating from the United States. Led by South Carolina, eventually eleven southern states would secede from the Union. They formed their own republic and called it the Confederate States of America.

In the seceded South independent companies seized federal arsenals and installations. For example, the federal arsenal at Fayetteville, North Carolina,

was taken over and eventually became the center of Confederate firearms manufacturing. Among the forts taken over was Fort Pulaski protecting the approaches to Savannah and Fort Moultrie at Charleston. The guns of South Carolina volunteer artillery companies were used first to threaten and then bombard Fort Sumter in Charleston Harbor.

When the Civil War began, the regular army numbered a little over 15,000 men. Most were scattered at isolated frontier outposts. In order to protect the capital and put down the southern rebellion, President Lincoln ordered 75,000 men into federal service for 90 days to put down the rebellion that threatened the union's existence. This would be the first of several federal calls for volunteers that eventually brought 2.8 million men into the army. An additional 1.1 million served in the Confederate army. In an effort to meet increased manpower needs, each side instituted a draft. The northern draft resulted in riots in Wisconsin, Indiana, and New York. In July 1863 violence erupted in New York City, and federal troops had to be called in to restore law and order. In the process over 1,000

rioters were either killed or wounded. In the Confederacy the draft was universally disliked, but it was not met with the same violent opposition as had occurred in the north. Both sides then unceremoniously dropped conscription as a method of raising troops. Therefore, the bulk of the soldiers that fought on both sides were volunteers. The nuclei of both armies were formed by regulars brought east and by antebellum independent military companies.

The Southern surrender in the spring of 1865 signaled a rapid and massive demobilization. Within six months, nearly 800,000 federal volunteers were mustered out of the service. Several hundred thousand ex-Confederates returned to their homes as well. The Regular Army was sent back to frontier outposts, to fortresses protecting ports and harbors and into the South to help with its reconstruction.

After nearly five years of hardship, sacrifice, and carnage, Americans had their fill of war and the military. With the war over and no serious threats on the horizon, men turned to peaceful pursuits and activities. In the North, the militias all but ceased to exist.

Charge! With sabers drawn and moving at the extended gallop, when about 50 yards from the enemy, the leader commands - CHARGE! Troopers push their mounts to full speed, cheering and waving their sabers wildly in the air. At the gallop, a horse is traveling between 25 and 30 m.p.h. Onlookers in carriages watch as the troop pushes the charge home. *OHS-Hayes*

Horseshoer at work in the field. Notice the various horseshoes hung on the tree to the left of the smithy. The leather-apron-clad smithy is standing in front of a portable field forge. The next customer patiently waits his turn, c. 1900. *WRHS*

Mounts were brushed and curry-combed at least once a day. Horses were given water before feeding. The daily horse ration for Troop A mounts was nine pounds of oats, 14 pounds of hay, and five pounds of straw. Horses were not to be worked after a full feed. Soldiers are wearing a white canvas fatigue or work uniform. C. 1900. *WRHS*

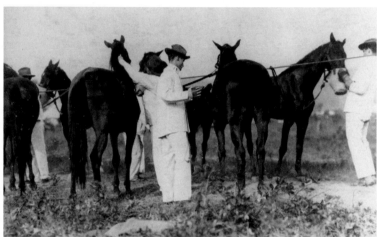

Ohio's Adjutant General reported in 1869 that the entire ordinary militia of the state was just two infantry companies and two batteries of artillery. In the years after the Civil War many independent companies were dissolved.

## INTERVENING IN LABOR DISPUTES

The period 1865 to 1877 marked a low period for the volunteer citizen soldier. That was about to change.

During the summer of 1877 an event took place that had not previously happened in the United States. A national strike was called by dis-gruntled workers.

The Great Railroad Strike of 1877 began on the Baltimore and Ohio Railroad in response to cuts in train-crew wages. Since the Panic of 1873 workers had been struggling to make ends meet. The railroad operators refused to recognize the workers' right to organize a union, and they were even more unwilling to negotiate with one. Frustrated and angry, railroad workers began disrupting train traffic and destroying railroad property. In an effort to stop the destruction of their property, the railroad owners appealed to the governors to call out their state

The Troop's second armory was built on the corner of Willson (East 55th Street) and Curtis Avenues. Members of the Troop personally borrowed $8,000 from Society for Savings to fund the building's construction. The inscription above the main entrance reads "Willson Avenue Riding School" and above the left first floor windows "First Cleveland Cavalry Armory." c. 1881. *OHS-Hayes*

Reception room. Willson Avenue Armory. c. 1890 *WRHS*

militias. In Maryland, Pennsylvania, and West Virginia some militiamen refused to obey the orders of their officers and went over to the strikers.

The strike spread from the Baltimore and Ohio to other railroads. Non-railroad workers, such as baggage and freight handlers, struck in solidarity. Soon the country was choked by a logjam of rolling stock. With the approach of autumn, the strike lost its momentum and the workers began to return to their jobs. Law and order had been restored by federal troops and "loyal" militia units. That summer nearly a hundred people lost their lives, and several hundred were injured.

The growing, largely foreign-born labor force with its tendency towards militancy in resolving grievances was perceived as a threat to the nation's well being. Cleveland and other northeastern Ohio cities had experienced a virtual explosion of unprecedented and unchecked industrial growth. Starting in the 1870s Cleveland's industrial expansion attracted a large number of workers from Eastern Europe, and by the end of the century there were nearly 32,000 Czechs, Poles, and Hungarians in the Cleveland labor force.

It's a man's world in the Willson Avenue armory club and reception rooms. Note, the Victorian opulence, trophies, and manliness of the furnishings, including the spittoons. Illumination is provided by gaslight fixtures. c. 1890 *WRHS*

Troopers are firing at targets on the indoor marksmanship range located on the top floor of the armory. Note the gaslight fixtures down the center of the gallery. Two large semaphore signal flags are mounted near the rear wall, along with fencing masks and chest protectors. c. 1890. *WRHS*

## THE FIRST CITY TROOP OF CLEVELAND

The city had gotten off lightly in the summer of 1877, but tensions between labor and management remained high.

Soon after the strike fizzled out, Cleveland civic and business leaders met to formulate plans to deal with future strikes. Events in Maryland, Pennsylvania, and West Virginia had demonstrated that some state militia troops could not be relied upon to obey the orders of their officers. In response to these unsettling events, local Civil War hero and businessman, General James Barnett, was given command of the city's "loyal" military companies. The oldest of the independent companies was the Cleveland Grays. Organized in 1837, the Grays had seen service during the Civil War and had survived the military doldrums that had followed. During the strike they were called to duty.

At the end of August 1877, another Cleveland Civil War general and business leader, Mortimer D. Leggett, outlined the concerns and apprehensions of the business community in a letter to Barnett. Leggett wrote that there was a serious problem as events in Maryland, Pennsylvania, and West

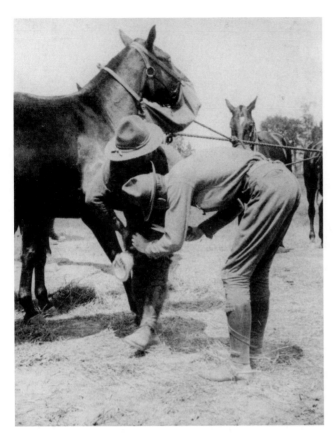

"A good trooper thinks first of his horse . . . ." At day's end horses and equipment were checked and cleaned. Particular attention was given to caring for the horse's feet. Troopers use "nippers" to remove ragged or uneven parts of the hoof. Note that the horse has on the feedbag. *WRHS*

At Camp Perry troopers hone their rifle shooting skills, firing from the bluffs into Lake Erie. *WRHS*

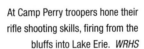

Virginia had illustrated. The ordinary or common state militia could not be trusted to do its duty. General Leggett's solution was to organize a reserve of loyal troops that could be counted on to reinforce the police in preserving order and protecting lives and property.

Throughout the country the Great Railroad Strike of 1877 brought about a dramatic shift in militia activity. In response to labor's lawlessness, states increased their military budgets and stepped-up recruiting campaigns. The response to General Leggett's call to arms was immediate.

Members of Cleveland's business and professional communities met in mid-September at Weisgerber's Hall on the corner of Prospect and Brownell streets to air their concerns over the labor strife that was rocking the country and to determine what could be done to control it in Cleveland. Other meetings followed, and on October 10, 1877, 41 young men chartered an independent volunteer cavalry company. Those present were members of the city's socio-economic elite. Like their comrades in the Grays, Cleveland's well-to-do cavalrymen would have no compunction about using a little force of their own

Public horsemanship competitions and exhibitions allowed troopers to show off their riding skills. Standing in the saddle, troopers "dress right." Onlookers can be seen in open windows and on front porches of houses in the background. c. 1900. *WRHS*

to subdue unruly union members. The name chosen for the new group was The First City Troop of Cleveland. Their first drill was held in early December at Weisgerber's.

In keeping with independent company traditions, the Troop promulgated by-laws and operating procedures. Included was an article delineating the Troop's dress uniform. The uniform was inspired by European light cavalry fashions. The officers and enlisted men's uniforms were described as a *chasseur* jacket of dark-blue cloth trimmed with black silk braid. Trousers were light blue cloth with a yellow stripe down the outer seam. Dress headgear was a black bear-skin busby. The custom-tailored uniforms were manufactured by Brooks Brothers of New York.

Early records indicate that annual dues were in the vicinity of $40. The cost of a good cavalry mount and the necessary equipment was around $90. The significance of the cost is made clearer when compared with the average income for Americans at that time of about $60 a month. At the time, factory workers toiled ten hours a day for around 20 cents an hour.

Membership in the First City

Wearing their dress uniforms, astride matching mounts, Cleveland's "Black Horse Troop" passes under a black crepe-draped arch during the funeral of President William McKinley in 1901. Canton, Ohio. *WRHS*

Troop of Cleveland was by invitation, and the application had to be endorsed by a member. The application was then read at a meeting, referred to the Elective Committee, and posted on the bulletin board for all to examine. If the applicant met all the "requirements," he was admitted to the company.

Not long after its organization the Troop organized a committee to find a suitable site on which to build their own armory. Land was purchased on Euclid Avenue between Sterling Avenue (East 30th) and Case Avenue (East 40th) almost opposite the present Masonic Auditorium.

The armory on Euclid Avenue served the troop well during its early years. However, the First City Troop soon outgrew its Euclid Avenue headquarters, and a lot for a new armory was purchased at the corner of Willson (East 55th) and Curtis avenues. Members of the troop, including Webb C. Hayes, Myron T. Herrick, and Jeptha Wade personally signed the $8,000 note from Society for Savings. The new armory included club rooms, stables, a rifle range, and a large drill area. A riding academy was also to be housed in the building.

Field kitchen is in operation during the St. Clairsville strike. Troopers carry metal mess kits and canteen cups from a chow line. Troopers in the background have already gone through the line and are making themselves as comfortable as possible before "chowing down." *WRHS*

## BURGEONING MILITARY ORGANIZATIONS

Shortly after the founding of the cavalry troop, the size of General Leggett's military reserve was increased when like-minded citizens organized the Cleveland Gatling Gun Company in June 1878. Armed with crank-operated machine guns, they joined the Grays, First City Troop, and two other companies, the Light Artillery and the Forest City Guards, as the loyal line against anarchy. In his annual message, Mayor William G. Rose boasted, "I have no hesitation in saying that the military organizations of this city are capable of affording ample protection to the lives and property of our citizens in case of danger."

Immediately after the Great Railroad Strike, Ohio and other states began to take measures to professionalize their militias. State legislatures began allocating funds for the purchase of equipment, training, and the building of new armories. It was during this time that the term National Guard came into general use when referring to state militias. Despite the increased military presence, violent strikes and labor agitation became a regular feature of the industrial north's long, hot summers.

During times of civil unrest, Ohio's cavalry was called upon to maintain order and protect property. In July 1922 Governor Harry L. Davis ordered the cavalry to curb lawlessness during a coal strike in Belmont County's St. Clairsville. Troop A bivouac with two-men "pup" tents. *WRHS*

The city reeled from the effects of two strikes in 1882 and 1885 at the Cleveland Rolling Mill Company. Workers struck for what have come to be known as the "bread and butter" issues of labor: better pay, shorter hours, and safe working conditions. The company answered by hiring "scabs" or non-union workers. Violence broke out as the new non-union men tried to make their way to the mill. Mayor Renssalaer R. Herrick placed the independent companies, including the cavalry troop, on alert. They remained in their armory awaiting marching orders that never arrived.

Two years later the "scabs" hired during the previous strike struck for the same reasons the men they replaced had. Before the end of the nineteenth century Cleveland would shudder under the effects of two more strikes. The Brown Hoisting and Conveying Machine Company Strike came in the summer of 1896, and the Streetcar Strike took place in 1899.

Business slowdowns caused by the Panic of 1893, plus efforts on the part of owners not to lower the dividends paid to their stockholders, forced the Brown Hoist and Conveying Machine Company to lay off 800

Troop A drawn up in line, await orders to take their place in the funeral procession of Cleveland industrialist and former U.S. Senator and "President-Maker" Marcus A. Hanna in February 1904. Cleveland, Ohio. *WRHS*

men at its Hamilton Avenue works. Violence erupted. In response, the Ohio National Guard's Fifth Infantry was called out and performed its duties in an exemplary manner. It reinforced the Cleveland Police Department and protected lives and property. The Fifth Infantry's conduct reflected the state's new commitment to military professionalism. The independent companies stood on guard at their respective armories.

Three years later, on June 10, 1899, a particularly nasty strike broke out when 850 workers of the Cleveland Electric Railway Company

walked off the job. The strike lasted longer and was more violent than most, and resulted in a great deal of property destruction.

Throughout the city, police and militia battled strikers and their sympathizers. Strikers erected barricades across tracks, started fires, attacked streetcars, and fired guns. On June 20 a mob of about 8,000 stormed the company's south side car barns on Holmden Avenue. As law and order broke down, Mayor John H. Farley called out both the National Guard and the independent companies.

Initially, Cleveland's cavalry troop was ordered to protect car barns and escort streetcars in the Broadway-Union neighborhood. The next day they were ordered to the West Side. At the intersection of Pearl and Clark streets a hostile crowd gathered as the troops approached. Soon the troopers were being pelted with bricks, bottles, and firecrackers. In response, the troopers were ordered to draw their sabers. Some of the horses became difficult to control, and one trooper went down with his mount. The troop charged the mob, and one man was wounded by a saber thrust. Violence soon declined, but there were still sporadic incidents until the strike was settled in September. Throughout the strike Cleveland's cavalry troop had performed its duties well. Organized labor accused them of being the tool of big business and vilified them as strike breakers.

Troop A escorts Marshal Foch's motorcade past chilled and rain-soaked onlookers in University Circle. The Wade Lagoon is seen just beyond the lead horseman, and the Art Museum is in the background. *WRHS*

25

Three-man pyramid. *WRHS*

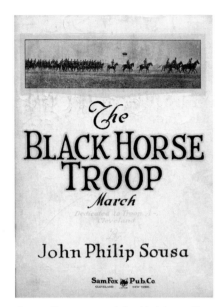

Because they were mounted on black horses, Troop A was known as the "Black Horse Troop." To commemorate his long friendly association with Troop A and to honor their service, John Philip Sousa composed "The Black Horse Troop March" in 1924. *CG*

## FIRST CITY TROOP BECOMES PART OF OHIO NATIONAL GUARD

In the late 1880s a measure was introduced in the Ohio legislature to place all military companies directly under state control. If passed, the state's independent companies, including the Cleveland Grays, Gatling Gun Company, the First City Troop, and others would have the choice of either joining the Ohio National Guard or disbanding. Before the legislature acted, on August 29, 1887, Cleveland's cavalry voted unanimously to join the Ohio National Guard. The First City Troop became Troop A, Ohio National Guard. The Cleveland troop joined three other cavalry troops already on the state rolls. Two of these troops had been independent companies before joining the National Guard. The 1st Troop of Cincinnati had been the Washington Dragoons and the 2nd Troop from Hillsboro was the Scot Dragoons. The proposed law was not passed by the legislature.

The militia laws were not changed until the passage of the federal Militia Act of 1903, the Dick Act, forced the dissolution of the remaining independent companies. Of the remaining independent companies, some joined

Polo is a fast, rough, and dangerous sport. Cavalry units fielded one or more polo teams. The First Cleveland Cavalry Blues competed against local and out-of-town teams. They were district champions in 1927. *WRHS*

Good horsemanship and guts. Jumping over an obstacle at the extended or full gallop. *OANG*

the National Guard, others were disbanded, and some simply became uniformed social clubs. Responding to the mandates of the Dick Act, the Forest City Guards and the Light Artillery chose to join the National Guard. The Gatling Gun Company remained active as a military social club until disbanded by the membership in 1905. The city's oldest independent company, the Cleveland Grays, did not become part of the National Guard or disband. The Grays continued their training and social activities and became a gentlemen's military social club. However, when the National Guard was mobilized for service on the Mexican border in 1916, the Grays volunteered and became part of the 3rd Ohio Volunteer Infantry. The Cleveland Grays have continued their social role to the present time.

Civil unrest continued into the twentieth century. Ohio cavalrymen were called upon many times to help maintain order and protect lives and property. A tobacco price war between Ohio and Kentucky growers necessitated calling up the cavalry in 1908. When coal miners went on strike in 1922 in St. Clairsville, the cavalry was called to help maintain order.

In November 1922, Marshal Ferdinand Foch of France visited Cleveland during a tour of the United States. Marshal Foch inspects Troop A. *WRHS*

On Halloween 1952 a riot broke out at the Ohio State Penitentiary in Columbus. While repairs were being made at the Columbus penitentiary, a portion of Camp Perry was turned into a temporary prison. Ohio's cavalrymen were assigned to the makeshift lockup as guards.

## CEREMONIAL AND SOCIAL INVOLVEMENTS

Since 1877 Ohio's cavalrymen have been on duty protecting lives and property and keeping law and order during all sorts of man-made and natural catastrophes. They have,

however, played a key role in more pleasant events as well. Ceremonial duties and social events were traditions established by the independent companies and later perpetuated by the National Guard.

The First City Troop of Cleveland immediately established a tradition of hosting an annual dinner to commemorate the anniversary of its founding. It also held joint competitions and social events with the Gatling Gun Company and the Cleveland Grays. Sumptuous banquets celebrating national holidays and local anniversaries became occasions for raising glasses

Flanked by an honor guard of troopers, President Herbert Hoover's car drives past the Halle Brothers Building as it heads down Euclid Avenue during his 1930 visit. Hoover, wearing a light-colored fedora, is seated in the right-side rear seat. *WRHS*

in numerous toasts. Parades, encampments, and military and sporting competitions were also organized. In summer 1879, a large crowd gathered at Cleveland's League Park to watch a baseball game between the Troopers and the Gatling Gun Company "Gunners."

Public horsemanship exhibitions allowed the cavalrymen to "show off" their prowess in the saddle to family, friends, and members of the community. Several times each year the cavalry troopers would put on mounted exhibitions or, as they were called, "Military Circuses." The Troop A Annual Exhibition and Games of 1908, for example, included competitive platoon drills, a pack-saddle race, rough riding (without saddle), riding double, vaulting to a second horse, pyramid riding (four horses and eight men), mounted wrestling, competitive head cutting (saber drill), stake pick-up at the gallop, a low-reach contest, and a novelty race. The events were judged by Ohio Volunteer Cavalry and Regular Army officers.

Before and after World War I, Ohio's cavalry troops competed against one another in horsemanship and military skills such as marksmanship.

In response to "Pancho" Villa's March 1916 attack on Columbus, New Mexico, President Woodrow Wilson ordered a general mobilization of the National Guard. Troop A escorted by members of the Veterans Association marched out of their Willson Avenue headquarters, past cheering crowds, down Euclid Avenue to the Union Depot. Their ultimate destination was the border with Mexico. *WRHS*

Each troop fielded one or more polo teams as well.

The sight of a cavalry troop escorting local dignitaries at various civic ceremonies fulfilled protocol requirements and awed onlookers. Cleveland cavalry troops were much sought after for escort duty. As they trotted down the street beside the carriage or automobile of a visiting dignitary, sabers drawn, wearing their hussar-style dress uniforms and seated on splendid black mounts, they must have been an impressive sight to see. In the nineteenth century and early twentieth century, Cleveland's "Black Horse Troop" acted as escort to a number of Ohio governors and United States presidents. They were invited to participate in the inaugurations of presidents Hayes, Garfield, Harrison, and McKinley. In 1897 Troop A sold a number of their black mounts to the Culver Military Academy in Indiana. To this day, Culver has a ceremonial black horse troop.

After World War I they provided escorts to Marshal Ferdinand Foch, General Pershing, and President Herbert Hoover. The First World War's Supreme Commander of Allied Forces, Marshal Foch of France,

Remounts were not considered completely trained until they could execute all that was required of them in the line of duty. They needed to be accustomed to firing, band music, the fluttering of flags, and all other sights and sounds peculiar to a martial environment. Bronco riding was but one aspect of the horse's training. Bronc riding along the Mexican Border in 1916. *WRHS*

A cavalryman's best friend was his horse. Putting on the "feed bag" along the border. Mount is saddled with a M1904 Mc-Clellan saddle. Trooper is armed with a M1903 "Springfield" bolt-action rifle and .45 caliber automatic pistol. *WRHS*

toured the United States as a guest of the American Legion in fall 1921. The Marshal visited Cleveland for two days. Cheering crowds greeted him as he was escorted up Euclid Avenue by Troop A, the 145th Infantry Regiment, and the 112th Engineers. Marshal Foch spoke to a crowd of over a thousand Legionnaires at B.F. Keith's Theater on Euclid Avenue near East 105th Street. Before leaving Cleveland, Western Reserve University conferred on Foch an honorary doctorate.

Six years later the American Legion sponsored a visit by General John J. Pershing. Thousands of jubilant onlookers turned out to see the General's motorcade escorted up Euclid Avenue by Troops A and G, the 112th Engineer Regiment, and the Cleveland Grays. The General spoke at the American Legion headquarters on East 21st and Euclid Avenue. He spent the night as a house guest of industrialist and troop alumnus Samuel J. Mather.

After watching the first game of the World Series between the St. Louis Cardinals and the Philadelphia Athletics, President Hoover visited Cleveland in early October 1930. The previous October the stock market crash had triggered the most ca-

The troop is patrolling along the Rio Grande. *WRHS*

lamitous economic catastrophe in American history - The Great Depression. As the economy spiraled downward seemingly out of control, the president came to Cleveland to address the 56th Annual Convention of the American Bankers Association at Public Hall. The assemblage of 11,000 bankers heard the president caution them to control the money supply and be "judicious in their extension of credit." The Cleveland Grays and Troop A provided the president's honor guard.

Not all ceremonial duties were happy occasions. The First City Troop of Cleveland also acted as honor guard at funerals of dignitaries and fallen comrades. Solemnly Troops A and G escorted the remains of their old comrade, Ambassador Myron T. Herrick, to his final resting place at Lakeview Cemetery. The ambassador to France and former Ohio governor was a troop member and very active in the Veterans Association. Among the dignitaries attending the ceremony was Colonel Charles Lindbergh. Two years earlier Ambassador Herrick had greeted him when he landed in France after making the first solo trans-Atlantic air crossing.

The army used airplanes, automobiles, trucks, and wireless communications for the first time during the 1916 Punitive Expedition. Many of the trucks were manufactured in Cleveland by the White Motor Company. Since the army did not have enough soldiers who could drive, White Motors was contracted to supply drivers as well. *WRHS*

## PROTECTING THE NATION

These honorary duties were not only a reflection of the cavalrymen's impressive appearance, but their status within the community. The National Guard, including Ohio's cavalry, had been created to bolster the regular army during times of national crisis. On many occasions, from the end of the nineteenth century to the present day, Ohio's cavalry has been called forth to help protect the country from foreign threats.

Cuba had been part of the Spanish Empire since the 1490s. At the end of the nineteenth century the Cubans

began a series of insurrections against their Spanish occupiers. The Spaniards fell upon the Cuban *insurrectos* with a tremendous ferocity. American public opinion, fueled by the yellow journalism of the Hearst and Pulitzer newspaper syndicates, began to pressure President William McKinley to use American power and influence on Spain to cease its brutal suppression of the insurrection, or perhaps even to grant Cuba its independence.

As a show of force and to protect American interests, President McKinley ordered the battleship *Maine* to Havana. Anti-Spanish sentiment

Machine guns, barbed wire and shell craters that rivaled the moon's surface were not conducive to cavalry operations. Subsequently, Ohio's cavalry was converted to field artillery. Cleveland's Troop A was sent to France as Battery A, 135th Field Artillery. Battery A is seen in formation in France. c. 1918. *WRHS*

33

A gun crew consisted of eight soldiers or artillerists. The gun commander, a corporal, is called the gunner. The seven privates servicing the gun are called cannoneers, No. 1 to No. 7. A gun crew from Battery A takes a break. To the left of the gun is the caisson or ammunition chest. The crew wears steel helmets and gas masks strapped to their chests for quick use. *WRHS*

Upon returning from France, Ohio's cavalry was reconstituted and designated the 107th Cavalry Regiment. In June 1923, Cleveland's cavalrymen occupied a spacious new armory home in Shaker Heights. *WRHS*

reached the boiling point, when on the night of February 15, 1898, an explosion blew the *Maine* to pieces killing 260 members of the crew. The cry for war against Spain rang loudly throughout the country.

Congress declared war on April 25, 1898. President McKinley ordered out the regular army and issued a call for volunteers. The members of Troop A and their Veterans Corps (in essence, the alumni association) successfully lobbied the McKinley administration and the War Department to ensure that Ohio's cavalry would be placed on

the roster of units called for action against Spain.

By early May the members of Troop A had recruited two additional troops and were ordered to report to Columbus. On May 4, Troops A, B, and C, carrying silk guidons made for them by the senior class of Hathaway Brown School, marched out of the Willson Street Armory and headed for the train depot. Cleveland's cavalrymen were accompanied by rousing marches and patriotic tunes played by none other than John Philip Sousa and his 60-piece band. Sousa was in town performing two concerts at Grays

In the years between the world wars, the 107th spent many annual summer encampments at Camp Perry. Established in 1908, Camp Perry is located near Port Clinton on the shores of Lake Erie. Moving cavalry units long distances was an arduous task. Special train cars had to be procured such as those seen from the Arms Palace Car Company. Arms also manufactured circus cars. *WRHS*

Detraining. Sometimes the horses cooperated and sometimes they didn't. *WRHS*

Armory on Bolivar Road. Members of the troop that knew him asked if he and his band could accompany them to the depot, and Sousa agreed.

The next day, Cleveland's Troops A, B, and C joined cavalry units from Cincinnati, Columbus, Dayton, Marysville, and Toledo and were mustered into the 1st Ohio Volunteer Cavalry Regiment. From Columbus, the 33 officers and 555 enlisted men of the Ohio cavalry proceeded to Chickamauga Park, Georgia. The army, however, found itself unprepared to feed, uniform, and equip the great number of troops that had rushed to the colors,

let alone transport them overseas. Ohio's equipment was slow in arriving; transport was delayed, and movement orders were countermanded.

Subsequently, the closest the Ohio cavalry got to the Spanish was Huntsville, Alabama. At war's end they were mustered out of federal service and returned to their status as state troops. Troop A resumed its duties in Cleveland and Troop B in Columbus. The others were disbanded. However, within a few years additional cavalry troops were recruited in Cincinnati and Toledo. The war with Spain had heralded a new era in American

Dismounted troop in line formation. Troopers are carrying the M1913 straight-blade "Patton" saber. The saber was so called because it was designed by George S. Patton, Jr., when he was assigned to the Mounted Service School at Fort Riley, Kansas, prior to World War I. *WRHS*

Cavalry drill regulations states that, "Clean horses . . . smartly turned out, add to the spirit of an organization and give a fair indication of its discipline and efficiency." Troop A had the cleanest and best groomed horses in the regiment. c. 1925. *WRHS*

Fatigue detail. Under the watchful eye of a corporal, a trooper is cutting grass the old fashioned way, one blade at a time. c. 1930. *OANG*

history and for the First City Troop of Cleveland. The United States had become a global power with global responsibilities.

In response to its newly acquired responsibilities, the U.S. Army set about to modernize itself. In order to effectively protect the nation as well as America's overseas possessions from its enemies, the army had to be reinforced by a well-equipped, well-trained, and well-led National Guard. The Militia Act of 1903, or the Dick Act, provided federal oversight for the training and equipping of the National Guard. The Dick Act, thus, standardized

the National Guard. Those independent companies that had been active in Ohio were given the option of joining the National Guard or disbanding.

As the Army and National Guard were modernizing, war clouds were gathering over Europe. On June 28, 1914, Archduke Franz Ferdinand of Austria-Hungary and his morganatic wife Sophie were murdered by fanatical Serbian nationalists during a visit to Sarajevo, the capital of Bosnia-Herzegovina. The archduke's assassination triggered the seminal catastrophe of the twentieth century, World War I.

From chaos there will be order. Troop setting up encampment at Camp Perry. c. 1925. *OANG*

There is an adage in the army, "There's nothing more dangerous than a Second Lieutenant with a map." Map reading exercise at Camp Perry. *WRHS*

As Europe's great powers squared off at one another, the official policy of the United States was to maintain its neutrality. That began to change, however, when on May 8, 1915, a German submarine torpedoed the British passenger liner *Lusitania*, bound for Liverpool from New York City. The ship sank with the loss of 1,153 lives, including 128 Americans. The event horrified Americans. Coupled with other unsettling developments, many Americans began to realize the fragility of their neutrality.

At the same time American relations with Mexico hit a new low. In 1910 a democratically inspired revolution broke out against the 34-year dictatorship of Mexico's Porfirio Diaz. The subsequent instability prompted President Woodrow Wilson to invoke the Roosevelt Corollary to the Monroe Doctrine. President Wilson's interference in Mexico's internal affairs, together with military provocations at Tampico and Vera Cruz pushed Mexican-American relations to the breaking point. On January 10, 1916, a Mexican bandit, revolutionary, and folk hero, General Francisco "Pancho" Villa, and his band stopped a train at Santa Ysabel in western

Troop on the march in double column formation. *OANG*

Regimental Commander, Colonel Dudley J. Hard, and his staff at Camp Perry. c. 1926. *WRHS*

Mounted saber drill. A melon stands in for an enemy soldier's head during a mounted saber attack. The mount is at a full gallop, traveling at about 25-30 mph. Camp Perry. c. 1926. *OANG*

Chihuahua Province and murdered 18 American mining engineers.

The following March, Villa and several hundred of his men crossed the border and attacked the town of Columbus, New Mexico. After a sharp fight with elements of the 13th Cavalry that were garrisoning the town, Villa and his men retreated back across the border. Twenty-four American civilians and soldiers were killed, as were nearly 80 of Villa's men.

President Wilson's response was immediate. He ordered "an armed force be sent into Mexico with the sole object of capturing Villa and secur-

ing the border." Within two days of Villa's attack, Brigadier General John J. Pershing, commanding 5,000 regulars, crossed the border in pursuit of Pancho Villa.

President Wilson mobilized the National Guard on June 18, 1916. Orders were issued the following day by Governor Frank Willis for Ohio Guard units to report to their armories for duty. Troop A and other units began recruiting drives. The Troop Veterans Association raised money for incidental expenses. Twenty-five "rookies" were signed up, and at a special luncheon

Troopers are firing .45-caliber automatic pistols while galloping at bobbing targets. *CSU*

held for the cavalrymen at the Union Club on Euclid Avenue, a check for $2,000 was presented to them "for the comfort and enjoyment of the men." Similar scenes were repeated throughout the city as young men came forward to enlist.

On the morning of July 4, 1916, Troop A left its armory on Willson Avenue on foot and marched down Euclid Avenue to the Union Depot. Acting as escort and marching at the head of the column were 75 members of the Veterans Association. Among the veterans were Charles C. Bolton, Sr., Myron T. Herrick, and Samuel

Mather. The next morning a *Plain Dealer* headline described the sendoff as "Society Weeps as Wealthy Sons Go Away as Soldiers."

Unfortunately, the scene at Columbus's Camp Willis was abysmal. The camp was poorly laid out, conditions unsanitary, and the rations unhealthy. All was made worse by an extremely hot summer.

In the service there is an adage, "rank hath its privilege." The same may be said of the relationship between wealth and privilege. While some National Guard outfits suffered terribly at Camp Willis,

During the summer of 1924, the commander of the 107th, Colonel Lathrop, desired to have the best band in the Ohio National Guard. He got his wish when the award-winning Fostoria High School Band temporarily became the 107th Cavalry Regimental Band. Under the direction of band director Jack Wainwright, Fostoria's young musicians donned military uniforms and went to Camp Perry for the annual summer encampment. *OANG*

The herald of things to come, tanks on maneuvers at Camp Perry. These are American-licensed copies of the French Renault M1917A1 tank. Operated by a crew of two, the tank could reach a maximum blistering speed of 9 mph. c. 1927. *WRHS*

As war clouds began to gather in Europe, the army began to modernize and reorganize itself. In August 1937 the 107th was ordered to Fort Knox, Kentucky, to summer training with cavalry units from other states and with Regular Army units. The 107th arrives at Fort Knox. *FCC*

Cleveland's Troop A was given privilege cards for Columbus's best hotels and private clubs. When given their army physicals, it was found that about half the men were overweight and over height for cavalrymen. After several well-placed telephone calls to Cleveland and to the War Department, the regulations were waived.

The First Ohio Cavalry Squadron entrained for Texas on September 1, 1916. Five days later the troopers pitched their tents at Camp Pershing on the outskirts of El Paso. At the end of October the Troop was ordered to

Fabens, Texas, for border patrol duty along the Rio Grande.

Patrols along the Rio Grande were ridden day and night to prevent the smuggling of arms and ammunition into Mexico. Ohio cavalrymen patrolled the border west to San Elizario and east to Fabens.

In addition to patrolling, mounted drills and competitions were held with other cavalry units. Regimental competitions were held in February 1917 to determine which troop in the regiment had most benefited from the training received on the border. Of the cavalry units in the contest,

Regimental bivouac at Fort Knox. M1934 pyramidal six-man squad tents have been erected. Note the wooden floors. *FCC*

Setting up the regimental encampment at Fort Knox. A squad from Troop A is putting up tents, while the remainder of the troop unloads the train. *FCC*

Attention and Present Arms! Regiment in retreat formation. Retreat is the formal lowering of the colors at the end of the work day. *FCC*

Cleveland's Troop A was awarded the Efficiency Pennant for receiving the highest number of points for "horse training and horsemanship." Michigan's Troop B took second-place honors. That evening Troop A invited the entire regiment to a celebration with music and beer. A couple of days later, Ohio's cavalry received orders to withdraw from the border and return home.

From Texas, the Troop proceeded to Camp Benjamin Harrison in Indiana. On February 28, 1917, they were mustered out of federal service. The Troop reached Cleveland three days later with 33 government mounts, three wagons, and some "smuggled" burros. A week of celebrating sponsored by the Veterans Association followed.

Pancho Villa was never captured, but the army and the National Guard received valuable field training which would serve them well within the next year. During the Punitive Expedition, the army used automobiles, airplanes, and trucks for the first time. Ironically, it was also the last horse cavalry campaign in U.S. Army history.

To the continuation of Germany's unrestricted submarine warfare

Standing inspection. Members of Troop B are inspected for their soldierly appearance and the cleanliness and serviceability of their weapons and equipment. *FCC*

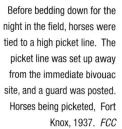

Before bedding down for the night in the field, horses were tied to a high picket line. The picket line was set up away from the immediate bivouac site, and a guard was posted. Horses being picketed, Fort Knox, 1937. *FCC*

campaign was added the threat of a German alliance with Mexico. The interception of German Foreign Secretary Arthur Zimmerman's telegram to his ambassador in Mexico suggesting the alliance was the final blow to America's commitment to neutrality. It moved President Wilson to ask Congress for a declaration of war against Germany. In his war message of April 2, 1917, a somber President Wilson said, "It is a fearful thing to lead this great peaceful people into the most terrible and disastrous of all wars, civilization itself seeming to be in the balance."

Aggressive recruiting campaigns were again begun. The Ohio National Guard was tasked to raise an entire division of nearly 28,000 soldiers. Technology had transformed the nature and conduct of warfare. The machine gun, rapid-fire artillery, and barbed wire made a war of maneuver impossible. Within months of the war's start, a line of barbed-wire-protected trenches and dugouts snaked its way across Europe from the Swiss border to the North Sea. Separated by the infamous "no man's land," the soldiers on both sides of the conflict endured infinite discomfort. Advances

Policing up after chow. Troopers stand in line to dip their mess kits in garbage cans full of boiling water. Fort Knox, 1937. *FCC*

Guard duty. Squad of troopers marching to guard posts. *FCC*

How many troopers does it take to load a field kitchen onto the back of a pack horse? Fort Knox, 1937. *FCC*

measured in hundreds of yards were made at the cost of thousands of lives. Europe's elite cavalry formations had been all but decimated.

The American Expeditionary Force being sent to France would have little use for cavalry. Some cavalry units would remain in the United States to patrol the border with Mexico. Most of the others would be converted to field artillery units. In a last attempt to deploy to France as cavalry, Troop A's commander traveled to Washington, D.C., to speak directly with Secretary of War Newton D. Baker. Secretary Baker's answer was straight

forward, "Change to field artillery." Ohio's cavalry regiment was converted to field artillery at the end of May 1917.

Field artillery batteries needed twice as many men as a cavalry troop. Using the catchy slogan, "Ride to War with A," another aggressive recruiting campaign got under way. In total, three field artillery regiments were raised for Ohio's division. After some preliminary training, Ohio's "rookie" artillerists proceeded to Camp Sheridan near Montgomery, Alabama, where the 37th Division (The Buckeye Division) was being organized and trained. Ohio's field artillery units

Animals picketed, evening chow and duties over, the men of Troop A take a break after a long day in the field. Fort Knox, 1937. *FCC*

Marksmanship qualification at the rifle range. Soldiers had to qualify or shoot at and hit targets at least 40 percent of the time at distances of 200 to 1,000 yards. A hit at the center of target was marked as a "Bull's Eye." A miss was signaled by waving a red flag nicknamed "Maggie's Drawers." Firing line with targets is seen in the distance. Fort Knox, 1937. *FCC*

were designated the 134th, 135th, and 136th Field Artillery Regiments respectively. Cleveland's Troop A became Battery A, 135th Field Artillery.

The 135th was organized into six batteries and armed with 75-mm field guns. Each battery had four field pieces and two anti-aircraft machine guns. In addition to 1,500 men, provisions were made for the care of 726 draft horses, 442 riding horses, and 154 draft mules. Training consisted of artillery drills, digging trenches, first aid practice, physical training, gas drills, signaling, and semaphore communications. Officers attended

classes taught by French field artillery officers. Topics included: fire control, cover and concealment, constructing battery emplacements, and gas defense. After nearly nine months of intense and rigorous training, the regiment left for France in the middle of June 1918.

Upon its arrival in France, the 135th was sent to artillery camp near Bordeaux for extensive training in firing French 75-mm guns, gaining familiarity with French horses, and continuous practice in range firing. Six weeks later the regiment moved to the front.

A break on the firing line, troopers wait for orders. *FCC*

A rolling field kitchen serves "dinner" to troopers at the rifle range. Trooper kneeling in the foreground is holding a canteen. *FCC*

Field telephones connected range officers and spotters to the butts. Butts were deep trenches under the targets where work crews scored hits or misses and changed targets, Fort Knox, 1937. *FCC*

Ordered to the Marbache Sector near the town of Atton, the regiment's mission was to provide artillery fire support to the 92d Infantry Division. From Atton the regiment moved to positions in the Troyon Sector of the St. Mihiel Salient to provide fire support to the 33rd Division (Illinois National Guard). Most of the regiment remained in this position until the Armistice in November.

The regiment spent five more months in France before boarding the battleships *New Hampshire* and *Vermont* at Brest. After two weeks at sea they arrived in Newport News, Virginia, in March 1919. Within a month the 135th Field Artillery was mustered out of federal service. Discussions and meetings were held for the immediate reestablishment of Ohio's cavalry.

The First Ohio Cavalry reappeared on the state's roster of troops on October 25, 1920. The unit was changed to the 107th Cavalry Regiment on July 1, 1921, with headquarters in Cincinnati. In 1923 Cleveland's cavalry unit moved out of their old Willson Avenue armory into a new spacious, modern facility at Fairhill and Kemper Roads on the Cleveland-Shaker Heights

In 1940 the 2nd Squadron's horses were replaced by M3 armored scout cars, originally designed and built by Cleveland's White Motor Company. Armor plating was supplied by Diebold Company of Canton. It was armed with two .30 caliber and one .50 caliber machine guns. It could carry seven soldiers plus the driver. The M3 is exhibited on the Mall behind the Cleveland Public Library. The Terminal Tower can be seen in the background. *CSU*

While the U.S. is not yet directly involved in World War II, troops are being readied for eventual service, and here are headed for Camp Forrest, Tennessee, February 1941. *Clink*

border. The two-story structure had headquarters offices, club rooms, and stables. In addition, a civilian riding academy was housed in the facility. As with the previous two armories, this one too was the property of the Cleveland Cavalry Veterans Association. Several more reorganizations followed, and in 1929 the regimental headquarters was moved from Cincinnati to Cleveland.

Summer training encampments were held along Lake Erie's shore at Camp Perry near Port Clinton, Ohio. During the summer of 1933, the 107th participated in joint ma-

neuvers with units from Kentucky, Massachusetts, and Rhode Island. The following year Fort Knox, Kentucky, hosted maneuvers designed to determine the future of horse cavalry operations. The army was modernizing. For the cavalry modernization meant mechanization.

The cavalry branch underwent some drastic changes in the decades following the First World War. The challenge of the shock of the charge to break the enemy's line became the responsibility of the nascent Tank Corps. Horse cavalry reconnaissance was replaced by troopers riding in

Scout cars are lined up opposite wooden barracks at Camp Forrest. Each had space for a platoon of soldiers and was heated by a coal-fed furnace, February 1941. *Clink*

IDENTIFICATION CARD
NATIONAL GUARD OF THE UNITED STATES
ARMY OF THE UNITED STATES
*This is to certify that:*
DONALD J. CLINK
ACTIVE NATIONAL GUARD
IV-V-40
IS ENLISTED IN TROOP B 107TH CAVALRY
I CERTIFY THAT THE ABOVE-NAMED MAN IS ENROLLED IN THE NATIONAL GUARD OF THE UNITED STATES UNTIL DATE INDICATED ABOVE.
No. 88
WILLIAM A. WEAVER CAPT. 107TH CAV., COMMANDING

National Guard identification card. *Clink*

During maneuvers at Camp Forrest, a trooper draws a bead on the "enemy" with an M1928 Thompson submachine gun or "Tommy gun." *Clink*

fast-moving, well-armed scout cars or mounted on motorcycles.

The Versailles Treaty which ended World War I was just two decades old, when the rebuilt German army stunned the world on September 1, 1939, with an attack on Poland. Fast-moving columns of tanks and mechanized infantry supported by mobile artillery and dive bombers made quick work of Polish defenses. The following spring the Germans repeated their Poland success against the Low Countries and France. The German General Staff had developed a doctrine of warfare designed once and for all to prevent a bloody repetition of the stalemate of World War I's trench warfare. They called it *blitzkrieg* or lightning war. Americans realized that it would only be a matter of time before the nation would be a war.

From 1939 to 1941 President Franklin Delano Roosevelt and Congress took measures to step up rearmament. Congress passed the Selective Training and Service Act of 1940, the first peacetime draft in United States history. Regular Army and National Guard training and reorganizations were increased.

By 1942 all the horses had been replaced by motorcycles, jeeps, and scout cars. On maneuvers in California. *CSU*

In convoy formation, scout cars break for lunch in Delaware, Ohio, February 1941. *Clink*

Ohio's cavalrymen spent three weeks of summer 1940 on maneuvers at Wisconsin's Camp McCoy. That November the regiment was reorganized and received the designation 107th Cavalry Regiment (Horse/Mechanized). The 1st Squadron continued to be mounted on horses and the 2nd Squadron was equipped with scout cars and motorcycles. Simultaneously, the 107th was joined by elements of the 22nd Reconnaissance Squadron.

National Guard units were being mobilized for one year of federal service. Camp Forrest, near Tullahoma,

Tennessee, was to be the regiment's home for the next year. The 107th was ordered to active duty on March 5, 1941. Over the next year the regiment participated in maneuvers in Tennessee, Louisiana, and the Carolinas. The Japanese attack on Pearl Harbor on December 7, 1941, catapulted the United States into World War II, joining the Allies in the war against the Rome-Berlin-Tokyo Axis.

Shortly after the declaration of war, the 107th was ordered to Fort Ord, California. For the next three months it manned positions and conducted patrols along the California

Repulsing an imagined Japanese invasion. Maneuvers on the west coast. c. 1942. *OANG*

Battlefield technology advanced by leaps and bounds during the Cold War. Helicopters were added to the regiment's inventory in the late 1950's. Originally assigned to the Chardon airport in Geauga County, eventually the Aviation Troop was moved to the Akron-Canton Airport. 107th aviators stand next to an OH-23 Raven helicopter. *OANG*

coast from Carmel north to the Golden Gate. They were looking for any signs of Japanese submarine activity, saboteurs, and fifth columnists. The regiment received a not-unexpected jolt in spring 1942 when the U.S. Army took away its horses. The horse cavalry in the United States Army was officially consigned to history. All cavalry units became fully mechanized.

Between August and December 1942, Ohio's troopers underwent desert training at Camp Young, California. This was followed by more beach patrols and reorganizations. On New Year's Day, 1944, Head-

quarters and Headquarters Troop (HHT) was designated as HHT, 107th Cavalry Group; the 2d Squadron as the 107th Cavalry Reconnaissance Squadron, and the 1st Squadron as the regular army's 22nd Cavalry Reconnaissance Squadron.

At the beginning of 1944, the 107th Cavalry Group Headquarters was assigned to Fort Polk, Louisiana. In early summer 1944, the 107th Reconnaissance Squadron moved to Camp Hood, Texas, and participated in training for overseas deployment. The 22nd Reconnaissance Squadron was inactivated on August 15, 1944 at

An M88 "Hercules" tank recovery vehicle prepares to tow a disabled Patton tank. The tank weighs 52 tons. Hence, the nickname "Hercules." *OANG*

Barracks cleaning or a "G.I. Party." c. 1962. *CSU*

In the 1950's tanks became a lethal addition to the cavalry regiment's arsenal. 107th M48 "Patton" tanks on a training exercise at Fort Knox, Kentucky. In the background a rifle squad has emerged from the rear of an M113 armored personal carrier. c. 1965. *OANG*

Camp Gruber, Oklahoma. The personnel were reassigned to the 3323rd Signal Information and Monitoring Company and sent to the Third Army in Europe.

After completing overseas training, the 107th Reconnaissance Squadron sailed from New York and arrived in France in the middle of January 1945. Initially assigned to the 66th Division (Black Panthers), in April they were transferred to the 103rd Division. The 107th conducted numerous reconnaissance and security missions during spring and early summer 1945 in both Germany and Austria. After Germany's

surrender in May 1945, troops and equipment began to be shifted to the Pacific in preparation for the anticipated invasion of the Japanese home islands. The 107th was ordered to the Pacific Theater and was en route to the Philippines when the war ended.

The 107th Cavalry Group Headquarters was inactivated in March 1945 at Camp Polk and the 107th Cavalry Reconnaissance Squadron at Camp Bowie, Texas, eight months later. At war's end the army reevaluated its strengths and weaknesses and made the appropriate decisions to meet future challenges. By the late

"Rise and shine!" Each soldier was issued a shelter half. Two halves equal one "pup" tent. c. 1962. *OANG*

Troopers on a mine clearing exercise at Camp Grayling. c. 1970. *OANG*

An M113 armored personnel carrier is on maneuvers at Camp Grayling, Michigan. Introduced in 1960, the original battle taxi was designed to move soldiers toward an objective. The lightly armored vehicle protected the 13 soldiers inside from small arms fire and shrapnel. When the objective was reached, the soldiers emerged from a ramp at the rear of the vehicle. The M113, extensively used in Vietnam, is still in service today. c. 1970. *OANG*

1940s the 107th Cavalry Regiment was returned to Ohio's active unit roster.

The Second World War was not yet over when cracks began to appear in the Grand Alliance. An undeclared Cold War began as the world divided between democracies led by the United States and communist states dominated by the Soviet Union. The threat of a third world war was always present as both sides created arsenals of atomic weapons capable of destroying every living thing on the planet many times over.

Greatly outnumbered by Soviet and Warsaw Pact armored divisions in Europe, the United States countered by placing additional armored divisions and cavalry regiments on its National Guard rolls. Several more reorganizations took place as the regiment was transformed from a mechanized cavalry reconnaissance organization to armored cavalry. Now equipped with tanks, the regiment possessed greater firepower and battlefield flexibility.

Only once was the regiment issued a federal "warning alert." In fall 1961 relations between the United States and Soviets became severely strained when the East Germans attempted

Troopers suiting up in their gas masks and protective hoods during a chemical attack training exercise at Camp Grayling, Michigan. c. 1972. *OANG*

Firing the Light Antitank Weapon or LAW at Camp Grayling. c. 1975. *OANG*

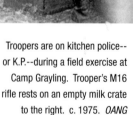

Troopers are on kitchen police--or K.P.--during a field exercise at Camp Grayling. Trooper's M16 rifle rests on an empty milk crate to the right. c. 1975. *OANG*

to close the East-West Berlin Sector borders, first with barbed wire and then with a concrete wall. In response to Soviet support of the East Germans, President John F. Kennedy authorized a United States-NATO alert. A preliminary alert order was issued to Ohio's armored cavalrymen, but tensions eased before activation orders had to be given.

## CIVIL UNREST

Although tested in the theaters of war and the menace of the Cold War, people were ill prepared to deal with the urban rioting and anti-Vietnam

War protests of the 1960s and 1970s. The violence of the great wars had been fought across the seas. The urban and campus conflicts brought the violence home.

Fed up with broken promises and the slow pace of the Civil Rights Movement, many young African Americans broke with the nonviolent and integrationist views of Martin Luther King, Jr., and violently demanded immediate equal rights and black power.

Beginning in the mid-1960s race riots came to characterize what became known as "the long hot

Movement to the suburbs, plus the necessity to have a more modern space to store and maintain equipment necessitated building a new armory for the 107th. The Shaker Armory was sold to the Cleveland Skating Club, and a new armory was built in Warrensville Township (Highland Hills) in 1970 and named in honor of former regimental commander, Woods King. *FCC*

Exhibit promoting the 107th and the National Guard is on display at Maple Heights Home Days at Southgate Shopping Center, c. 1974 *OANG*

summers" in most Northern and West Coast cities. The most famous riot occurred in the Watts neighborhood of Los Angeles, California. Ohio, however, was not spared as the Hough Riot and the Glenville Shootout erupted in Cleveland.

On a hot, humid July evening in 1966 rioting broke out on Cleveland's east side when the white bartender at the 79'ers Bar on the corner of East 79th Street and Hough Avenue refused a black woman a drink of water. Fueled by past racial insults and injustices, the news spread fast. Soon a crowd of over 300 people

gathered at the intersection. The Cleveland police arrived on the scene and ordered the crowd to disperse. The order was met by a shower of bottles and rocks. Gunshot-like sounds were heard. The police replied in kind, and the Hough Riots erupted for the next six nights.

Unable to control the crowds, fire bombings, and sniper attacks on police and fire fighters, Mayor Ralph Locher called for help from the National Guard. Governor James Rhodes ordered units of the 107th Cavalry Regiment to Hough. The Regimental Headquarters, Headquarters Troop,

Mobilized for State Active Duty, 107th Cavalry troopers prepare to move to Cleveland's Hough neighborhood for riot duty, July 1966. *CSU*

Headed for Hough, troopers ride aboard a 2 1/2 ton truck, July 1966. *FCC*

Troops A, B, and C of the 1st Squadron and Headquarters Troop, Troops E, F, and G of the 2nd Squadron, plus the 2nd Battalion of the 145th Infantry Regiment were placed on State Active Duty. The orders given to the 107th's commander were clear and succinct: ". . . You are hereby ordered to assist police to maintain law and order, to prevent looting and protect life and property." Troopers first reported to the Kemper Road armory. There they were issued field equipment and weapons. They were also given their marching orders.

When the lead elements of the 107th arrived at the Cleveland Police Department's mobile command post at East 79th Street and Hough Avenue, unruly people were throwing rocks and bottles and smashing store windows. There were numerous arson fires, and firemen and policemen were being injured. All this was accompanied by the occasional sounds of gunshots. Looting occurred wherever police were not present. The situation was deteriorating. In an effort to prevent further lawless behavior, Mayor Locher ordered the city's saloons closed.

Many Hough residents tried their best to ease tensions, and even brought baskets of food and cold drinks to patrolling Guardsmen, July 1966. *CSU*

A Jeep patrol is stopped in front of a storefront house of worship, July 1966. *FM*

Though initially hampered by a lack of transport, by midnight of the second day guardsmen began arriving in force. Seven hundred and twenty-five guardsmen were committed to action. Duties included foot patrols, mounted roving patrols, stationary posts, control of key intersections, and protection of firemen responding to alarms. Fire trucks moved in convoys, protected by an armed cordon of police and guardsmen. These actions immediately reduced the number of violent incidents.

Civilian traffic into the neighborhood was blocked. An after-dark curfew was enforced. Fires, looting, and other general acts of lawlessness lessened. The police and guardsmen were also helped by two days of severe thunderstorms. The Hough Riot began to lose its momentum.

Gradually, the guardsmen were released from duty. On Sunday morning, July 31, 107th Cavalry jeep patrols on Hough's streets were replaced by Cleveland Transit System buses. City services were restored to the neighborhood. Mayor Locher's request for the National Guard was deemed to have been "prudent, proper and correct." Tragically, four people were killed,

Cleveland Police walk past an abandoned house set on fire by vandals, July 1966. *CSU*

A 107th Cavalry jeep patrol speeds by the smoldering ruins of a building destroyed by arsonists during the Hough disturbance, July 1966. *CSU*

National Guardsmen and Cleveland police were posted on east side Rapid Transit bridges, July 1966. *CSU*

many were injured, and millions of dollars of property was destroyed. The 107th Cavalry learned some valuable lessons that would serve them in good stead two years later when another east side city neighborhood exploded.

The social climate remained inflamed. Black leaders such as Stokely Carmichael openly called for armed resistance to societal oppression. Metropolitan police forces were likened to armies of occupation. African Americans and their neighborhoods were viewed as victims of just another form of white colonial oppression.

In 1968 Cleveland's East Side again became the scene of a violent confrontation between black militants, the Cleveland police, and the Ohio National Guard. More violent than Hough, the Glenville Shootout, as it came to be known, would take nine lives, wound 14 other individuals, start 34 fires, and do $2.6 million in damage.

City officials had been forewarned that militant civil rights activist and self-proclaimed astrologer Fred "Ahmed" Evans and his followers were in possession of illegal automatic weapons and that they were in the

Two years after the problems in Hough, the 107th was placed on State Active Duty when lawlessness erupted during what came to be known as the Glenville Shootout. Troop A jeep patrol and Cleveland police provide protection for firemen and their equipment. Glenville, July 1968. *CSU*

107th Regimental Commander, Colonel Dana Steward and staff officers go over operational plans. Glenville, July 1968. *CSU*

mood to use them against their "oppressors." Evans later admitted that he had used grant monies earmarked for neighborhood social projects to purchase arms and ammunition. His goal was to foment race war in Cleveland. Evans's plan also included the assassination of Mayor Carl Stokes, other civic leaders, and Cleveland policemen.

In an attempt to calm the situation, Councilman George Forbes met with Evans at his Glenville neighborhood headquarters. Evans told Forbes that he was angry over an eviction notice he had received for failure to pay rent

and because he was under Cleveland police surveillance. Two Cleveland surveillance units were watching Evans and his band. Evidence suggests that Evans's activities were also being monitored by the FBI.

On the evening of July 23, 1968, a Cleveland Police tow truck was dispatched to pick up an abandoned automobile. Tow truck drivers wore uniforms similar to those of the police, but actually they were unarmed civilian employees of the department. As the crew began working, Evans and his men began firing at them. While never proven, there is strong evidence

Mayor Carl Stokes goes on television to brief the community on the situation in the Glenville neighborhood, July 1968. *CPL*

Jeep patrols were armed with M1 rifles, with bayonets fixed, and a .30 caliber machine gun, Glenville, July 1968. *FCC*

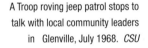

A Troop roving jeep patrol stops to talk with local community leaders in Glenville, July 1968. *CSU*

that the abandoned car and the shooting of the tow truck crew was a ploy to lure more Cleveland policemen into the neighborhood for an all-out battle.

Soon after the tow truck ambush, Evans and between 15 and 20 other black militants were in a shootout with the Cleveland Police Department. An angry and hostile crowd of young black men soon gathered. Empty police cars became the targets of firebombs. Along Superior Avenue in the vicinity of East 105th Street, windows were broken, businesses looted, and fires set. Fire trucks responding to real and false alarms were met by fusillades of

rocks and bottles, and in some cases, gunfire. The situation was spinning out of control. Shortly after midnight on Wednesday, July 24, Mayor Stokes asked Governor Rhodes for National Guard assistance.

National Guard units from all over the state were ordered to Cleveland. The headquarters and both squadrons of the 107th were mobilized and joined other Guard units in Glenville. The 1st Squadron took up positions near East 105th Street and Wade Park Avenue. As they had two years earlier in Hough, the 107th established mounted roving jeep patrols, manned

A burned-out TV station wagon, July 1968. *CSU*

Cleveland firefighters are silhouetted against a building set ablaze by arsonists, July 1968. *CSU*

stationary points, set traffic check-points, and again provided protection to firemen answering alarms. Fire trucks were accompanied by 107th jeeps mounted with .30 caliber machine guns.

At about 2:00 in the afternoon on that same day, Mayor Stokes made a controversial decision to have all white policemen and the National Guard units withdrawn from the riot-torn neighborhood. A six-mile area was cordoned off. The perimeter was to be guarded by white Cleveland policemen and National Guard troops. Patrols inside the boundary line

would continue, but these would be the work of black civic and religious leaders and black Cleveland policemen. While white offers were angered by the mayor's decision, no subsequent deaths were reported, and there was a decrease in looting that night. The following night the cordon was lifted, and regular police and guard patrols resumed.

By Saturday the riot had run its course and began losing momentum. Late in the day guardsmen were released from duty, police shifts returned to normal, and Glenville's streets were opened to traffic.

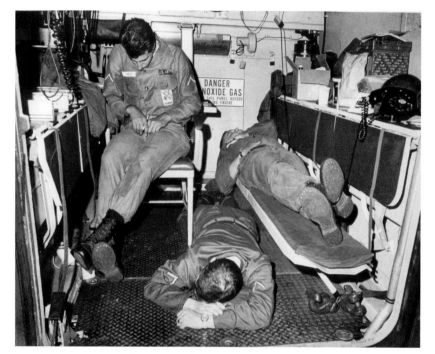

A G. I. can fall asleep any-where. Catching a snooze inside an M577 tracked com-mand post during the Glenville Shootout. July 1968. *CSU*

National Guardsmen are billeted in the Cleveland Convention Center during the Glenville Shootout. July 1968. *CSU*

Five black militants were eventu-ally charged with murder and found guilty, including the leader, Fred "Ahmed" Evans.

## CAMPUS UNREST
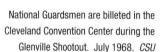

During mid-July 1968, Evans's war in Glenville replaced the Vietnam War on the headlines of Cleveland's newspapers. Still, news of the war and the protests against it were not far from anyone's attention. Since the Tet Offensive of 1968, the war in Vietnam had been growing increas-ingly unpopular among Americans, especially draft-age college students.

The American and South Vietnamese incursion into Cambodia in spring 1970 seemed to signal an escalation of the war rather than the "peace with honor" promised by President Rich-ard M. Nixon during his campaign for the presidency. The Cambodian invasion resulted in a nationwide rash of protests on college and university campuses. Violence frequently erupt-ed as militant protesters battled with police and national guardsmen who sought to quell it.

Students at Kent State University in Kent, Ohio, held a massive dem-onstration on Friday, May 1, 1970, on

National Guardsmen and snow fences cordon off the ruins of the burned-out ROTC building at Kent State University. The building was the target of arsonists during an anti-Vietnam War demonstration on Saturday evening May 2, 1970. The incident set into motion the events that led to the May 4th shootings. *KSU*

the "Commons" area of the campus center. Anti-establishment, anti-Nixon, and anti-war passions ran high as organizers called for more protests on the following Monday, May 4.

That Friday evening an unruly crowd gathered in downtown Kent's business district. Downtown Kent was a mix of small stores, restaurants, and bars that generally catered to the student population. Exactly how a "typical" Friday night deteriorated into a violent confrontation between students, non-students, anti-war protesters, and the Kent police is unknown. Beer bottles and rocks were

hurled at police, bond fires were set on downtown streets, windows were shattered, and stores were looted. Kent's mayor, Leroy Satron, declared an emergency and asked the governor to call out the National Guard. Governor Rhodes ordered the 2nd Squadron, 107th Cavalry and Companies A and B, 1st Battalion, 145th Infantry to Kent.

The 2nd Squadron had been activated the previous week for duty during a teamster strike. Shots were being fired at trucks traveling on the interstate highways and the Ohio turnpike. The 2nd Squadron had been

Demonstrators on the Kent Commons chant, jeer, and taunt National Guardsmen. Shortly before noon on May 4, the Guard gave order for the demonstrators to disperse. *KSU*

activated to patrol the highways and man bridge outposts. In response to Mayor Satron's call for help, the 107th troopers were reassigned to riot duty in Kent.

When the National Guard arrived in Kent on Saturday, May 2, they were greeted by a large crowd of protesters and a burning Reserve Officer Training Corps (ROTC) building. An estimated 1,000 demonstrators surrounded the burning building and began pelting police and firemen with rocks and other missiles as they attempted to bring the fire under control. A fire hose was

slashed by protestors. As the situation further spiraled out of control, at around 10:00 p.m. the National Guard entered the campus grounds. They were immediately confronted by demonstrators. The guardsmen responded with tear gas.

By Sunday morning nearly 1,000 National Guardsmen and their equipment occupied the campus. During the day, Governor Rhodes personally toured the campus. At a press conference he took a tough stance against the agitators. He likened student demonstrations to extreme revolutionaries and said

Bayonets fixed, Guardsmen prepare to advance on the demonstrators. *KSU*

107th Troopers, wearing gas masks, advance toward demonstrators on the Commons in front of Taylor Hall. *KSU*

that their violent behavior would be met by force. As nightfall came, the campus was rocked by more wildness as rocks, bottles, and tear gas canisters filled the air. Preparations were going forward for the next day's mass demonstration on the "Commons."

Despite a University order prohibiting any further demonstrations, a crowd began to gather on the "Commons" on Monday morning, May 4. By noon the crowd had swelled to around 3,000. The Guard made the decision to disperse the protestors. A jeep attempting to announce the dispersion order was pelted by rocks and forced to withdraw. A guardsman riding in the jeep was injured. Except for their steel "pot" helmets, the national guardsmen wore no protection. The already tense situation on the Commons escalated to a level of rage.

Guardsmen again began firing tear gas grenades at the crowd. Because it was a windy day, the gas dissipated and did not have the intended debilitating effect. As the mob chanted "Pigs off Campus," rocks filled the air, and some of the bolder protesters picked up tear gas canisters and threw them back at the soldiers. With the situation

Troopers, followed by news-men, fire tear gas as they continue their advance towards Taylor Hall. Demonstrators began throwing tear gas bombs back at the Guardsmen. *KSU*

worsening, the order was given to "load and lock" their weapons. The tear gas had failed to disperse the protesters. With bayonets fixed and weapons loaded, the Guard began to advance on the crowd.

Seventy-seven soldiers, or roughly two platoons from A Company and G Troop respectively, were ordered to advance on the crowd. As the soldiers advanced, the protestors moved out of the Commons and up what was called Blanket Hill and down the other side. The guardsmen followed the crowd up, over, and down the hill, but became disoriented by a chain link

fence. Screaming and rock throwing reached a crescendo. The guardsmen began retracing their steps back up the hill.

In an instant, 29 of the 77 turned and fired their weapons. Some fired into the air or ground, others directly into the student protestors. Sixty-seven rounds were fired in 13 seconds. Four Kent State students were killed and nine wounded in the fusillade. Most of the rounds were fired by Troop G. In statements made later, guardsmen said that no orders to fire were given. The firing had been a spontaneous reaction to the terrifying

Guardsmen clear the Commons in front of Taylor Hall. The Guardsmen crested Blanket Hill and then moved along the downward slope to the point where they opened fire. *KSU*

situation that had developed on the Commons and spread over to Blanket Hill. Nevertheless, 40 years later the tragedy at Kent State continues to be an emotional and controversial topic of discussion.

## NATURAL DISASTERS

Ohio's Troop A was founded as a response to the domestic emergencies created by the labor strife of late nineteenth and early twentieth centuries. Many times in the last century the 107th Cavalry was called to state active duty to protect property and preserve peace and order

and public safety. Ohio's cavalrymen have also answered the call to help their fellow citizens during times of natural disaster.

The 107th has provided relief assistance to Ohio communities devastated by natural disasters. The deadliest tornado in Ohio history struck Lorain and Sandusky on June 28, 1924. In Lorain, businesses and homes along 35 city blocks were damaged or destroyed. There were 85 people killed, 72 in Lorain. Governor A. Victor Donahey ordered 1,500 guardsmen, including Troop A, to the area. Troop A was sent to Lorain to

Damaged sign announcing May 9 Campus Day events that never took place. The day-long festivities were to have concluded with a concert by B.J. Thomas, David Frye, and Gary Puckett. *KSU*

patrol the streets, to prevent looting, and to assist in rescue work.

Ohio's cavalrymen have also provided aid to flood-ravaged areas of the state and during severe winter weather. Such was the case during the Blizzard of '78. In January and February 1978 a severe blizzard ripped into Ohio and virtually crippled the state. Governor Rhodes ordered the National Guard to provide assistance to stranded motorists and property owners. National Guard armories were turned into emergency shelters. Units of the 107th Cavalry, including HHT, Troop G, 2nd Squadron, and

HHT and Troop L, 3rd Squadron were mobilized. In each case the troopers provided material assistance to stunned residents and assisted local police in maintaining order and providing disaster relief.

The most destructive hurricane in the nation's modern memory occurred in August 2005 when the entire Gulf Coast region was devastated by Hurricane Katrina. In response to the catastrophic loss of life and property, elements of the 2nd Squadron, 107th Cavalry Regiment were sent to Lake Charles, Louisiana, to assist with relief efforts.

The crowded and traffic-congested market place of Jalula, Iraq, faces west from the police station main entrance, 2004. *OANG*

## REORGANIZATION AND A NEW ARMORY

Throughout the 46 years of the Cold War, the 107th Cavalry was maintained in a constant state of readiness. In 1956 the 2nd Battalion's Tank Company received an efficiency award for superior performance. Two years later the Tank Company was awarded the prestigious Eisenhower Trophy for excellence in training. The 107th Cavalry was a major early deployment element in support of North Atlantic Treaty Organization (NATO) contingency plans should war break out in Europe.

During the early 1960s the Cavalry Veterans Association sold its Kemper Road headquarters to the state of Ohio. In 1971 the 107th moved to the new Woods King Armory on Green Road in Warrensville Township. The Kemper Road armory was sold to the Cleveland Skating Club.

The decades of the 1960s and 1970s were periods of change and reorganization for the Ohio National Guard. Ohio's legendary 37th "Buckeye" Division was deactivated in 1968.

The collapse of the Soviet Union in 1991 marked the end of the Cold War and the need for an expensive multi-

Third Platoon of C Company, 1st Battalion, 107th Cavalry on a "potato" patrol. Patrols lasted three to four hours, with the Guardsmen wearing a protective vest, helmet, ammunition pouches, and other equipment in 100-degree weather - "baking like a potato." 2004. *OANG*

million soldier army. Subsequently, the early 1990s saw the closing of military installations and the deactivation of units. It was estimated in 1992 that the Defense Department planned to eliminate more than 140,000 reservists and National Guardsmen. Among those slated for elimination was the 107th Armored Cavalry Regiment.

Active guardsmen and many members of the Cavalry Veterans Association on September 1, 1993, gathered at North Canton Armory, near the Akron-Canton Airport to watch the colors of the 107th Armored Cavalry Regiment furled, cased, and

retired. It was an emotional and sad event. However, while no longer a separate independent command, the 107th designation was not lost.

Under the new U. S. Army Regimental System the old regiment became part of the 37th Brigade, 28th Infantry Division. In September 1994 the 1st Battalion and 2nd Squadron of the 107th became part of the 38th Infantry Division.

## CONTINUED INTERNATIONAL CONFLICT: KOSOVO AND IRAQ

The demise of the Soviet Union may have ended the Cold War, but

new international challenges quickly took its place. The 1990s were highlighted by the globalization of violence and terror on a scale not known since the darkest days of World War II. The death of Marshall Tito cleared the way for the breakup of Yugoslavia, and the resurgence of militant Serbian nationalism. The butchery that followed gave rise to a new metaphor - ethnic cleansing. President George H.W. Bush sent American troops to the Balkans to protect the newly created Macedonian Republic should it be attacked by Serbia or threatened by Greece.

In an attempt to end Serbia's persecution and "cleansing" of the Kosovo region's Slavic Muslims, NATO forces were sent in as peace keepers. In September 2004 units of the 38th Division were assigned to NATO's Multinational Brigade (East). The Brigade was composed of troops from Denmark, Finland, France, Greece, Lithuania, Poland, Ukraine, and the United States. Their mission in Kosovo was to lend stability to peace-making efforts, foster democratic institutions, and promote economic growth.

The 2nd Squadron, 107th Cavalry deployed its Headquarters and Troops

Finding caches of rockets, artillery shells, and other ordnance was a daily occurrence. Every item discovered, defused, and destroyed was one less potential Improvised Explosive Devise to be used against Coalition and Iraqi government forces. 2004 *OANG*

C Company commander meets with local government officials and Iraqi tribal sheiks to discuss democratization progress, peace, and public works. 2004 *OANG*

A, B, and C as Task Force Lancer. The troops were billeted at Camp Bondsteel near the town of Viti/Vitina in southeast Kosovo. Ohio's peacekeepers remained there until March 2005.

Terror struck America's shores on September 11, 2001, when two highjacked passenger aircraft were deliberately crashed into the twin towers of New York City's World Trade Center and a third was crashed into the Pentagon. President George W. Bush rallied the American people behind him to wage a "War on Terror."

It was public knowledge that Iraqi dictator Saddam Hussein encouraged and supported terrorist activities directed at the United States and its allies, notably Israel. Evidence gathered by the Central Intelligence Agency seemed to verify that the Iraqis were hiding "weapons of mass destruction." United Nations weapons inspectors had been allowed to return to Iraq after being expelled four years earlier, and they were reporting that the Iraqis seemed to be cooperating with them. Nevertheless, Saddam Hussein's history of rewarding suicide bombers' families with cash bonuses, his smuggling, and violating United Nations mandates

Hearts and minds. Troopers hand out candy to children in Jalula. 2004. *OANG*

led the Bush-Cheney administration to conclude that his denial about possessing "weapons of mass destruction" was another lie in a long series of untruths and suspect behavior. President Bush declared Iraq a threat to Middle Eastern stability and to America's safety and implemented his newly proclaimed doctrine of preemption.

American forces, accompanied by allied coalition troops, launched a "blitzkrieg-style" invasion of Iraq on March 20, 2003. Within 41 days of sometimes heavy resistance, the Iraqi army was defeated and Baghdad occupied. After going into hiding for nine months, Saddam Hussein was captured. Neither the destruction of the Iraqi Army nor Saddam Hussein's capture ended America's duties and responsibilities in Iraq.

Regular Army, Army Reserve, and National Guard units that participated in Operation Iraqi Freedom would have the responsibility of insuring the creation of a new Iraqi government based on democratic principles, of preventing factional violence, and of rebuilding the Iraqi economy.

Company B, 1st Battalion, 107th Cavalry was alerted for deployment

Young Iraqi girls, with their new American friends, smile for the camera, 2004. *OANG*

to Iraq on August 16, 2003. From its armory in the Cleveland suburb of Highland Hills (formerly Warrensville Township), the company moved to Fort Bragg, North Carolina. At Fort Bragg, Ohio's Guardsmen were attached to the 30th Armored Brigade of the North Carolina National Guard.

The troopers arrived in Kuwait at the end of February 2004. Before crossing the Iraqi border, they received training in urban warfare and in cordon and search operations. At the end of training, Company B's troopers moved to Kir Kush. During the next three months Company B conducted

over 60 convoy missions and operated a traffic control checkpoint. While conducting operations, the cavalrymen came under enemy fire on ten different occasions. They were moved to Baghdad's Green Zone in early June and provided escorts to convoys running to and from the Baghdad Airport, Balad, and Kir Kush. Other units of the 107th were also conducting operations in Iraq.

Company C, 1st Battalion, 107th Cavalry was assigned to Forward Operating Base Cobra three miles outside of Jalula. Jalula is in northeast Iraq, approximately 100 miles north

of Baghdad and 30 miles from the Iranian border. The battalion oversaw the implementation of democratic practices, manned traffic control checkpoints, and conducted joint day and night patrols with Iraqi national guardsmen and police. One trooper recalled, "Finding an improvised explosive devise was almost a daily occurrence for those on patrol."

## CONCLUSION

Since the First Ohio Cavalry volunteered for active service in 1898 to the 21st century deployments of the 107th Cavalry to Iraq, Ohio's cavalrymen have been a major part of America's frontline forces.

The mission of the National Guard remains to bolster the Regular Army in times of national emergency, to protect property and lives during local outbreaks of lawlessness, and to assist people when natural disasters strike. They are part of the community that they serve.

Since its founding as a an independent volunteer military company, the troopers of the First City Troop, Ohio Volunteer Cavalry, 135th Field Artillery Regiment, 107th Cavalry Regiment, 107th Armored Cavalry

In their off duty hours, troopers built a pavilion with a stone floor. The flag of North Carolina honoring the 30th Armored Brigade and the burgee of Ohio honoring the 1 Battalion of the 107th Cavalry have been paved into the floor. *OANG*

Headquarters and Headquarters Troop, 1/107th begins to celebrate their return from Iraq. 2004. *OANG*

Regiment, and 1st Battalion and 2nd Squadron 107th Cavalry, 38th Infantry Division--no matter what they have been called or how they have been organized--have performed all duties asked of them and met all challenges placed before them.  Throughout its 130-year history the troopers of the 107th Cavalry have displayed personal courage and selfless, honorable service to the citizens of Ohio, the United States, and to the Constitution that they have sworn to "preserve, protect and defend."

# U.S. ARMY ORGANIZATIONAL COMPONENTS

The fighting components of the U.S. Army are divided into fire teams, squads, sections, platoons, companies, brigades, divisions, and corps.

**FIRE TEAM.** This component of a squad is composed of four soldiers, and consists of a fire team leader, a grenadier, and two riflemen. It is commanded by a corporal.

**SECTION / SQUAD.** A squad consists of 8 to 16 soldiers commanded by a sergeant.

**PLATOON.** A platoon numbers 16 to 44 soldiers, and it is commanded by a first or second lieutenant, assisted by a platoon sergeant. It is composed of several squads. An infantry platoon has four squads. Tank platoons are called sections, two sections of two tanks each.

**COMPANY / TROOP / BATTERY.** This is a unified tactical unit that can perform battlefield functions on its own and consists of 60-200 soldiers. It is made up of three to four platoons and 15-25 vehicles. It has a headquarters platoon to carry out administrative functions and is generally commanded by a captain with the assistance of a first sergeant.

**BATTALION / SQUADRON.** This unit of 300-1,000 soldiers is tactically and administratively self-sufficient, thus capable of independent operations of limited duration and scope. It is composed of two to six companies, commanded by a lieutenant colonel and assisted by a command sergeant major. Air and armored cavalry units are called *squadrons*.

**BRIGADE / GROUP / REGIMENT.** A brigade has 1,000-10,000 soldiers, thus a large unit that can be deployed independently or semi-independently. Special Forces and Ranger units are called *Groups* and in the cavalry a *Regiment*. Composed of three or more battalions, it is commanded by a colonel.

**DIVISION.** A division has 1,000-10,000 soldiers and performs major tactical operations and sustained engagements. It is composed of three to five brigades. It is numbered and categorized by type - i.e. 37th Infantry Division, 2nd Armored Division, 1st Cavalry Division, 82nd Airborne Division. It is commanded by a major general, assisted by two brigadier generals, one each for maneuver and support functions. It is composed of three maneuver brigades and a support/service brigade.

**CORPS.** The corps has 20,000-40,000 soldiers and serves as the deployable level of command required to synchronize and sustain combat operations. Composed of three to five divisions, it is commanded by a lieutenant general, assisted by a command sergeant major.

All units larger than a corps are generally given the name "army." Armies are commanded by a lieutenant general and assisted by a sergeant major and a large staff.

*Source: Schading. A Civilian's Guide to the U.S. Military. (2007).*

# DISTINGUISHED UNIT INSIGNIA

## DESCRIPTION

Or, on a bend gules between a Roman Sword in sheath point to base
and a prickly pear cactus both vert, three alerlons of the field.

## SYMBOLISM

The shield is yellow for Cavalry.  The bend charged with the alerlons, taken from the
arms of Lorraine, is representative of World War I service and is red to indicate that the
107th Cavalry served as Field Artillery during World War I.  The Roman Sword in sheath
is for Spanish-American War service and the cactus for Mexican Border duty.

## ORIGINALLY APPROVED

8 March 1927 for the 107th Cavalry Regiment

## MOTTO

"FACERE NON DICERE"
(To act, not to speak)

# CURRENT ORGANIZATIONS WITH 107TH CAVALRY LINEAGE

A/1-148 INFANTRY REGIMENT
(WALBRIDGE)

C/1-148 INFANTRY REGIMENT
(TIFFIN)

D/1-148 INFANTRY REGIMENT
(SANDUSKY)

HHC/1-145 ARMORED REGIMENT
(STOW)

B/1-145 ARMORED REGIMENT
(CLEVELAND)

C/1-145 ARMORED REGIMENT
(STOW)

D/1-145 ARMORED REGIMENT
(NEWTON FALLS)

HHT/2-107 CAVALRY REGIMENT
(HAMILTON)

A/2-107 CAVALRY REGIMENT
(XENIA)

B/2-107 CAVALRY REGIMENT
(LEBANON)

C/2-107 CAVALRY REGIMENT
(GREENVILLE)

HHC/237 SUPPORT BATTALION
(CLEVELAND)

A/237 SUPPORT BATTALION
(CLEVELAND)

B/237 SUPPORT BATTALION
(YOUNGSTOWN)

G/237 SUPPORT BATTALION
(MEDINA)

D/128 SUPPORT BATTALION
(HAMILTON)

F/128 SUPPORT BATTALION
(ALLIANCE)

1192 ENGINEER COMPANY
(NEWTON FALLS)

FSC216 ENGINEER BATTALION
(WOODLAWN)

684 MEDICAL COMPANY
(COLUMBUS)

DET 1, 1485 TRANSPORTATION COMPANY
(DOVER)

1487 TRANSPORTATION COMPANY
(EATON)

A/1-137 AVIATION COMPANY
(COLUMBUS)

B/1-137 AVIATION REGIMENT
(COLUMBUS)

D/1-137 AVIATION REGIMENT
(COLUMBUS)

B(-)/3-238 AVIATION REGIMENT
(NORTH CANTON)

C/1-174 AIR DEFENSE ARTILLERY REGIMENT
(BELLEFONTAINE)

585 MP COMPANY
(DELAWARE)

838 MP COMPANY
(YOUNGSTOWN)

*Source: 1st Cleveland Cavalry Association*

# BOOKS, ARTICLES, PAMPHLETS AND THESES

Capodarco, Michael E.
*107th Mechanized Cavalry
Reconnaissance Squadron 1940-1941.*
2001. http://107thmechcavsqd.ieasysite.com/

Casper, Sherree, SPC.
*Story1. Listserv message, July 6, 2004.*
Lillian P. Sydenstricker@us.army.mil.

___ *Story2. Listserv message, July 6, 2004.*
Lillian P. Sydenstricker@us.army.mil.

Cleaver, Jason E.
*Breaking Point: Police Error and
Misconduct and the Glenville Riot.*
MA essay, John Carroll University, 2005.

Cleveland City Directory 1877.
Cleveland: Robinson and Savage Company, 1877.

Clink, Donald J.
*107th Cavalry ONG, 1941-1944.*
2005. http://www.donclink.com/
107th_Cavalry/index.html.

Cox, Kurt Hamilton and John P. Langellier.
*Longknives: The U.S. Cavalry and Other
Mounted Forces, 1845-1942.*
London: Greenhill Books, 1996.

Cunliffe, Marcus.
*Soldiers and Civilians:
The Martial Spirit in America, 1775-1865.*
Boston: Little, Brown and Company, 1968.

Doubler, Michael D.
*Civilian in Peace, Soldier in War:
The National Guard, 1636- 2000.*
Lawrence, Kansas: University Press
of Kansas, 2003.

Ellis, John.
*Cavalry: The History of Mounted Warfare.*
New York: G.P. Putnam's Sons, 1978.

Ellis, Wilbur R.
*Yellow Ribbon of Ohio: The Story of Ohio Cavalry.*
Cleveland: Unpublished, Date Unknown.

First Cleveland Cavalry:
*Fundamental Armory Training Regulations.*
Cleveland: 1936.

First Cleveland Troop.
*Constitution and By Laws.*
Cleveland: October 10, 1877.

Geer, Harold A.
*A Trooper's Scrapbook.*
Ravenna, Ohio: 1966.

Hill, Jim Dan.
*The Minute Man in Peace and War:
A History of the National Guard.*
Harrisburg: Stackpole Company, 1964.

Katcher, Philip, and G.A. Embleton.
*The American Indian Wars, 1860-1890.*
London: Osprey Publising, 1977.

___, and Ron Volstad.
*U.S. Cavalry on the Plains, 1850-1890.*
London: Osprey Publishing, 1985.

___, and Jeffrey Burn.
*The U.S. Army, 1892-1920.*
London: Osprey Publishing, 1990.

Langellier, John P.
*Fix Bayonets: The U.S. Infantry From the
American Civil War To the Surrender of Japan.*
Philadelphia: Chelsea House Publishers, 2000.

Letter from Colonel John Williams to
Colonel Edward Norwick.
Essex Junction, Vermont: February 28, 1998.

Masotti, Louis H., and Jerome R. Corsi.
*Shootout in Cleveland: Black Militants
and the Police, July 23, 1968.*
New York: Bantam Books, 1969.

Mewitt, Alfred.
*A Brief History of Troop A.*
Cleveland: Private Printing, 1923.

Moss, James A.
*Infantry Drill Regulations: United States Army 1911.*
Menasha, Wisconsin: George Banta Publishing Company, 1911.

___. *Manual of Military Training.*
Menasha, Wisconsin: George Banta Publishing Company, 1917.

*Official Roster of Ohio Soldiers
in the War with Spain, 1898-1899.*
Columbus: Edward T. Miller Company, 1916.

Patty, Clay W., and William F. Ball.
*A Brief History of the First Cleveland Cavalry:
Composed of Troops A and B, 107th Cavalry
Regiment, Ohio National Guard.*
Cleveland: Private Printing, 1937.

## BOOKS, ARTICLES, PAMPHLETS AND THESES *(continued)*

Revere, Paul.
*Cleveland in the War with Spain.*
Cleveland: United Publishing, 1900.

Rose, William Ganson.
*Cleveland: The Making of a City.*
Cleveland: World Publishing, 1950.

Rottman, Gordon, and Ron Volstad.
*U.S. Army Combat Equipments, 1910-1988.*
London: Osprey Publishing, 1989.

Schading, Barbara.
*A Civilian's Guide to the U.S. Military.*
Cincinnati: Writer's Digest Books, 2007.

Task Force Falcon, 38th Infantry Division Yearbook:
*September 2004-March 2005.*
Skopje, Macedonia: STV Prizna, 2005.

Troop A, Ohio National Guard.
*Constitution and By Laws.*
Cleveland: May 12, 1902.

Vourlojianis, George N.
*The Cleveland Grays:*
*An Urban Military Company 1837-1919.*
Kent, Ohio: Kent State University Press, 2002.

## PUBLIC DOCUMENTS AND REPORTS

City of Cleveland. Office of Mayor Carl B. Stokes.
*Chronological Report of Events*
*From 2:30 PM Tuesday, July 23 to 8:30 AM Sunday, July 28 On*
*Glenville Area Disturbance.*
Cleveland: 1968.

Headquarters and Headquarters Troop,
107th Armored Cavalry.
*S-1 Daily Staff Journal, 23-28 July 68.*
Cleveland: July 23-28, 1968.

State of Ohio. Adjutant General's Department.
*The Report on the Role of the Ohio*
*National Guard during the Hough Area*
*Riots in Cleveland 18-31 July 1966.*
Columbus: August 10, 1966.

___. *After Action Report: Blizzard '78.*
Columbus: March 28, 1978.

War Department. Office of the Chief of Staff.
*Cavalry Drill Regulations,*
*United States Army, 1916.*
Washington, DC: GPO, 1916.

___. *Provisional Drill and Service Regulations for*
*Field Artillery (Horse and Light).*
New York: Military Publishing Company, 1916.

___. *Manual for Stable Sergeants,*
*United States Army, 1917.*
Washington, DC: GPO, 1917.

## NEWSPAPERS AND MAGAZINES

*Armor Magazine*

*Buckeye Guard Magazine*

Cleveland *Plain Dealer*

Cleveland *Press*

New York *Times*

*Ohio Guardsman*

## INTERVIEWS

Blackford, Jason

Boehlke, Edward

Delau, Carl

Dixon, Lucian

Ehrman, George A.

Marinchick, Grant J.

Monastra, Nathan S.

Russell, Richard

Strasshofer, Thomas A.

Waser, Sidney R.

## ABOUT THE AUTHOR:

George N. Vourlojianis earned his doctorate in history, with specialization in 19th century American Studies, from Kent State University. He currently is associate professor of history at Lorain County Community College and campus advisor to the college's Phi Theta Kappa chapter. He also serves on the adjunct faculties of Kent State University and John Carroll University where he teaches upper-level history courses. In 1999 he received the Distinguished Teaching Award for Arts and Sciences at Kent, and in that year he was also designated a U.S. Military Academy Fellow. A previous book, *The Cleveland Grays: An Urban Military Company 1837-1919*, was published by Kent State University Press in 2002. He lives with his wife Sally in Elyria, Ohio.